To The New World

Carmelita McGrath

*For Lucy,
with best wishes,
Carmelita*

To The New World

Carmelita McGrath

St. John's, Newfoundland
1997

© 1997, Carmelita McGrath

Appreciation is expressed to *The Canada Council* for publication assistance.

All rights reserved. No part of this work covered by the copyrights hereon may be reproduced or used in any form or by any means—graphic, electronic or mechanical—without the prior written permission of the publisher. Any requests for photocopying, recording, taping or information storage and retrieval systems of any part of this book shall be directed in writing to the Canadian Reprography Collective, 214 King Street West, Suite 312, Toronto, Ontario M5H 2S6.

Acknowledgements

Several of these poems have appeared, some in slightly altered form, in *TickleAce*, *The Fiddlehead*, and *Room of One's Own*.

The author thanks the Canada Council, the Newfoundland and Labrador Arts Council and the City of St. John's for their support. Thanks to Gordon Rodgers for his insightful editing. Thanks to my family for their unwavering support.

∝ Printed on acid-free paper

Cover: Eve, 22.75" x 22". Wool on cotton. Kathleen Leah Knowling.

Published by
KILLICK PRESS
a Creative Publishers imprint
a division of 10366 Newfoundland Limited
a Robinson-Blackmore Printing & Publishing associated company
P.O. Box 8660, St. John's, Newfoundland A1B 3T7

Printed in Canada by:
ROBINSON-BLACKMORE PRINTING & PUBLISHING

Canadian Cataloguing in Publication Data

McGrath, Carmelita

    To the new world

    Poems

    ISBN 1-895387-77-9

I. Title

PS8575.G68T6 1996   C811'.54   C96-950220-6
PR9199.3.M42425T6 1996

*in memory of my grandmothers, Frances and Annie
for Hannah and Sonia
and for Leah, who leads us forward
through the generations*

Contents

Touring the Manor Houses	1
Annie, Telling Stories	2
Gone Girl	3
To the New World	4
Out of Place	14
State of Grace	17
The Half-Life of Taffeta	19
Sextet	21
Love and the Swan	28
Thinking about Washboards	29
Awake these Nights Dreaming in Colour	31
Adam and Eve on A Winter Afternoon	32
Aphrodisiacs for a Newfoundland Winter	34
Sprouting House	39
Floating	40
Guardian	42
The Way You Walk into the Water	44
three balloons on a wall	45
Among the Shadows of Everything	46
Early Acquaintance	49
Anthemic	51
de Chirico's girl doesn't sleep all night	52
How She Had Her Nervous Breakdown	54
For the First Time in Months, She Feels Her Feet	55
The Cat Is Dead; Long Live the Cat	56
If I Could Give You Now	58
Let Us Go and Find a Place of Worship	60
Breaking Ice	62
Dappled	63

Touring the Manor Houses

Excuse me, but I'd rather not see
another broad room
where stippled light
released through leaves reveals
the desk where he wrote that famous tract on natural history,
or that table where he pinned his creatures
and, watching the sky,
ordered the harvest begun.

Not again—please—
her garden room
where her hat hangs
in replica, where she sighed for the apple blossoms,
not her parlour
where her ghost still sits on the green divan,
warming its ankles by the fire.

Show me instead the kitchen,
the distance from the pump,
the slop buckets, the vessels of disposal,
the flatirons,
show me that low stone room where the laundry was done,
the sheets boiled, the pots where hares were simmered,
the small white attic rooms
where the women whose features I bear
unpinned their hair with reddened hands
and dreamt of lovers
coming to them over fields
of August hay.

Annie, Telling Stories

When her hat wore out, she turned it backwards, pinned the brim with a cabbage rose of second-hand organza; when that didn't work, she turned the hat inside out, revelling in the new felt, the wear and tear hidden in her hair.

When she needed coloured wool, she boiled some moss; after you feed and shear and card and spin and ball, what's a little extra effort, after all?

And when her daughter had first Communion, waiting upstairs were the old lace curtains—ready to become a veil. Annie bleached and starched, and then, pinned and tucked, and sewed the pleating when she got it right—add a crown of lily-of-the-valley, and you look as good as anyone.

And in summer when she'd come home from the flakes to see to dinner, there just wasn't enough time. So Annie (someone else told me) tied a rope around her waist. The other end was tied to the baby's cradle; she'd knead the bread and rock him with the rhythms of her labour, two actions synchronous, without interruption.

Gone Girl

Where is she?   still treading water?
gone girl who is not immortalized in a sad song,
who never traipsed the boggy streets of the new world,
or lived to cast her children like augural shells into the future.

How does she live now?   nameless
an entry in a literate man's journal,
a being of class and sex so different from her own;
she could not have looked the doctor in the eye,
yet he was the witness to her dying. In the end,
when morning broke and all he saw was grey horizonless water,
there was nothing to do but pen an entry
on her pain, and muse about the speed and nature
of the soul's evacuation.

How did she travel?   nameless
carrying da's old name, waiting to take on another,
she fell between names into a sea that, as soon as she set out,
had wracked her body, rent her sleep,
had begun to claim her.

How did she leave us?   nameless
never occupied a grave to lay a woman's claim:
a piece of land with her name on it; instead, a momentary rift
in that grey sheet of sea, then a closing over her,
lost between names, between continents.

How does she survive now?   nameless
his elegant hand could not record her
nor plumb the mystery of that disguised third trimester:
he could not possibly have known her.

To the New World

It is well known, sir, that food supplies here run very low in March...

Despair is the eater,
finding its snug place inside

cellular
the way the body lives, regenerates, dies

despair is the eater
in long winter months

when hunger upsurges
becomes a cloud that hangs over villages
when hunger speaks, becomes a word
darting from tongues obscenely, burning lips,
forcing everyone into silence
when hunger grows
a tough root or bulb, too bitter to eat
when hunger is born in March
in the guise of a baby girl
all her parents can think is
what to feed her?
all her mother can think
is whether to keep her.

We have been so long at sea, and yet seem far from any shore...

Waiting for birth is like waiting for migration,
like watching the sea:
sometimes in its plangent light you think you distinguish
the shapes of strange craft, strange creatures,
trying to imagine the unexperienced (the wind sings the word *coming*)
trying to imagine what sounds
their tongues will make, the colours of their eyes

and

waiting for birth is like watching the barrens for caribou,
and like walking for miles
through barren and marsh:
the back, the legs, the groin inflame
from walking on half-water, half-earth:
by sunset, you emerge in a clearing
where the light opens
onto a sparkling pond, and a fish jumps suddenly
halfway into the sky
and the wind sings of the dark coming:
too late to turn back.

It is an unpopulated place, rich in resources, where a hard worker might make a good life...

These stones are half-mute, some words extinguished,
...his wife Mary, aged 21 years, and son Michael, aged 1 day
...Elizabeth...27...
...and also Jane, 30, and daughter Faith, aged 6 months...

lichen owns the rest. This place

is built on bone
dream and bone.

> Two hundred years underground, Mary dreams of Harry's words in the first winter of their marriage. Landless, they would have land. And Harry spoke of boundless opportunity, of across the sea, seas so overpopulated the fish were waiting for someone to dip a net. She resisted. *Why would a place so rich be so unpopulous?* But he dreamed in her ears and her eyes and her mouth, dreamed in her vagina and the dreams entered her and took shape, became a son with a boat of his own, a daughter pulling from a tree the perfect worlds of russet apples.

> Elizabeth was joyous. She felt stronger, as if she'd left the cough far away somewhere. This new place rang with saws and hammers, air sang with wood and salt. She thought of opening a school, and of the eyes she'd felt on her back all summer. Impossible to think of hunger. And the cough crossing an ocean to find her.

Ah, Jane! To leave four boys and a slip of a girl behind with
William was all she thought of. Held the new one, named Faith,
in her arms and felt they were done for, yet at the last moments
the baby and Jane drew warmth from each other. And Jane, in
March delirium could look ahead, see the shining sun on waves
of summer. It was merely dreaming, like now when the sky
trembles and Jane knows ones related to her fly as on wings of
birds, city to city, over her.

Walk inland; beneath the trees that shelter this still place
lie more bones; walk shoreward;
in stone cairns lie other, earlier dreams.

Almost shipwrecked on dangerous shoals...

Birth is a search for the other
and a recognition,
dream made flesh

the baby is transverse breech
or as grandmother, the midwife,
would have said, *the poor thing is sideways*

the doctor borrows my dead grandmother's hands
and tries to turn the baby, cannot

we schedule surgery: he says
I'll be on my feet in no time. We say tomorrow,
better to do it before the holiday weekend.

At about four in the afternoon, we approached shore...

Birth is like the end of a long journey by sea. Before dark,
we approach a kind of shore and the air is different, the light intense.
The explorer is hauled ashore, screams at what she finds.

My grandmother, the midwife,
birthed a community
and turned her hands also
to washing and laying out the dead. Her hands
were a circle, holding life and tying the ends. Her dreams
were circular; at night what rose in her sleep—
frames of dipnets, arcs of rainbow, wedding bands.

A livyer asks what the voyage was like...

Afterbirth

after-the-birth

a month later and the doctor's right: my steps
are sure through the neighbourhood, and May is shining,
every voice I meet asks about the baby—

"What did you have?" a woman asks.
"A girl."
"I mean did you have a natural childbirth or an intervention?"
"A girl," I say. "A girl."

try to tell her about how I could have been caught
in one of grandmother's small circles, but the woman
lives in a new world, wishes for the old

hankers after candles, a house heated by wood,
her own root crops in winter, a flourbag strip
dusted with flour burned on the stove
tied around the stump of the baby's umbilicus

a simpler time, a safer time
more romantic than loving a soap opera hero
for those who have only an absence of memory
for March hunger
and small circles.

In 1997, a replica of the **Matthew** *will arrive to celebrate John Cabot's discovery of Newfoundland in 1497...*

well, that could have been his name
after he adopted Bristol
or Bristol adopted him; he wouldn't be the first
to change a name
for smoother sailing with the English

and his ship might not have been the *Matthew*,
might have carried
a name more feminine

to wherever it landed.

Consultants are having a hard time: where should
this replica-ship arrive? Cape Breton, St. John's, Bonavista?
Some say as south as Maine. The *Matthew* is lost at sea.

And no one knows a true thing about
John Cabot.
Or where he landed.

And many will not imagine what he discovered.

> On that June day when Cabot landed Somewhere, the people of Somewhere were already embracing the coast that was their source of food all summer. Fish and seabirds, seabirds' eggs, and in the dunes with the long sand grasses, the leaves of berries were already exhaling the scents of later seasons. The people of Somewhere called themselves *the people*, could not imagine this man of Bristol or Genoa, though some had dreamed of strange craft on the sea... could not imagine...

...nor can we. And where to land or what to celebrate?
O, make him real. (Make a commercial?) See Caboto,
small dreamer on the streets of Genoa.

By waters teeming with cod...

What can they be celebrating? Those fools in St. John's. All that money and not a hand's turn of work in it for anyone but consultants and committees. All a lot of foolishness and—look—they want to bring in more tourists to see—what? Replicas of this, replicas of that. Because the real thing is gone, is gone, my dear.

And they talk about the new economy. The information economy. The global economy. And it's like there's no room in this economy for people or jobs. You can't eat information.

And look at that plant, empty. Rusting. We used to be at the fish in that plant all day and all night. Now they say you can get a fish plant for a dollar—buy one if you got the nerve.

Sshh,
Mary wants to say.
This woman's talk disturbs
a two hundred year old dream
but her mouth is earth

so she lets the woman into her dream,
Harry's voice across an ocean
dreaming of fishes, riches

feels the tinder of the woman's anger,
tries to recall, but cannot,
a time when economies weren't global.

*What was once two days of rough walking, with
additional portions of the journey by horse and cart
and by train is now a two-hour Sunday drive...*

Birth is like a long journey by sea and then, at the point of exhaustion,
overland; years later
you are still tired yet strangely charged,
fierce with dreaming

everything you know you want to place in the child's hands

so that she can move among places, read maps
spot shoals, arrive home like a star at nightfall

I show my daughter the grave
of my grandmother of the circles, tell
of the birthing,
the laying out of the dead,
two washings with life in the middle

on this hill
the best view of the sea floods the land with a blue
that makes the green greener

this sea, dazzling thing;
sometimes in its plangent light
you think you distinguish the shapes
of strange craft, strange creatures

try to imagine the sounds their tongues will make,
the colour of their eyes.

Out of Place

Hard to place

that sense of longing
of or to or from
a place

longing most fervent

like wanting to know a twin who died at birth
or tasting again something consumed in a dream
or sensing in the air a wind from a place never visited
carried by a weather front and travel reading.

When her parents left the island
it was not
of their own accord but due to emptiness—

the neighbours all going, their boats
full
everything from tables to lamps to cleaning rags
houses towed
rafting across the bay
stillblue and beautiful

causing a miasma of forgetfulness (how it raged
in January melted away)
now in Toronto
her eyes cast on the word "resettlement"

in Canada's national newspaper,
another editorial advising the unemployed
to hop on another leg of the journey; she sees
a dot-to-dot complete-the-picture

large dots for large centres, at the end of the tracing
the word "Finish"

and she sees in her mind's eye houses of yellow and blue
crossing the Cabot Strait, sees
saltboxes with sails
mounting an invasion up the St. Lawrence.

In New York one day
she had seen the words "catchment centres"
written across the sky
and turned to see people swimming like fish
to openings that led them underground—

The age of her father as compared to the age of her mother: was that it?
Her father
twelve years older with an accent that droned like a single bee,
swearing he would die
if he had to move anywhere.
And did
but it took him eighteen years
during which he never let up complaining.
Her mother,
quick-stepper in a yellow and blue bandanna and turquoise stretchies,
butterfly floating toward the harbour and escape, towing
children behind her like swallowtails
dancing on the currents of her hands.

I'll break up with him, she thinks. Rather than go
to a farmhouse in the country. In the window of
a shop where the word "cappuccino" seems written across her face,
she rehearses, "I'm meant to migrate only to large places. Even
the Globe & Mail says so." And country meadows, though large,
are not in the cards.

Sometimes, in such shop windows, there's a ripple,
a change as if a stone has been thrown in water. The city clothes,
dark, aerodynamic, meant for swimming through human congestion
become a schoolgirl's summer rig, shorts patterned with watermelons,
and her eyes stare out from under bangs cut by her mother

who may be still travelling. The daughter imagines a bright bird,
from outport to small town to someplace like this,
glancing at headlines,
saying, "C'mon, we'll go." Always ready for a chance for excitement.

State of Grace

something so sublime about a white sweater
embellished with knitted flowers radiating
from small stones like pearls at their centres,
it smelled like the air that dried it with its breath.

something so clean about aunt's hand-me-down dress
white swiss dots on brown
sleeveless, trim of rickrack
this and the white socks, brown penny loafers
and hair that smelled of rain barrel.

any other day might find her
hiking up her grey school skirt
to make it shorter; rolling the waistband
into a tough defiant panel, practising
a song of strung-together curses,
smoking behind the school
fantasizing, all the fantasies somehow leaning
toward obliteration

*I will run off
with a grown man, and the family won't want to see me no more.*

it's an old notion: sin your way to freedom

but every second Saturday comes a time for the state of grace
trading a sin card for a penance card
all about dying, not living really,
grace was for when you died and needed it
a passport to the unknown country of eternity

you could go any night in your sleep...

She makes of herself a girl who would obviously be forgiven.

Born in original sin: what did that mean? Sins seemed so
terribly repetitive. If she had known who owned the sin, it
would have helped her. The event of her had soiled her mother
who had to be churched; she returns every second Saturday
to complete the ritual, make the forgiveness stick. No one has
taught her how to phrase the confession.

Excuse me for being born

might be a cliche, but as close to the truth as anything.

trying to figure out the subtleties of sins
of complicity and sins of omission,
at eleven, the girl wants to formulate
a lucid confession that will make the important things stand out.

She has just learned the word *lucid*;

it has something to do with light.

The Half-Life of Taffeta

You were adamant that I should have kept that dress,
danced in on New Year's Eve at the waterfront,
complemented by some gentleman's formal jacket,
swirling above legs wet from knee-deep snow.

I told you it was a size five,
would only fit half of me now,
gone green the way black does with age
like an old man's suit;
the boning that held the top up, did I tell you?
popped up and out one night while I was dancing,
my partner chortled: "She's wired, this one."

You pictured the dress
surviving in my daughter's dress-up trunk,
a costume, a put-on of her mother before she was one.

Kind of sad, I'll admit,
stuffing it in the green garbage bag
(it resisted crushing, kept puffing out as if alive):
it had gate-crashed, trespassed, high-stepped,
been worn with all the shoes danced to dust
across boundaries of countries, continents,
carried on ships, in cargo bays on planes
and once, just once,
squashed in a briefcase to a clandestine adventure
that, even now, only two people know about;

in its salad days, the dress crackled electrically
one night under a snowmobile suit
beneath snapping northern lights
on its way to the one formal dance of the year.

But surely taffeta survives somewhere,
must have a half-life like plutonium, invisible
but somewhere, making you and I
remember who we were, sending us on a wardrobe chase
to our former selves, who we were
on evenings when we wore gloves or smoked
long cigarettes, and believed like fanatics
in the power of champagne to show up at the right time.

Is there any of that left now?

the way the nights burned and glinted,
faceted as Murano glass, as bright
as moonbeams in old songs. And we fell silent;
on either side of the table, we were back,
hardly daring to tell stories hard to fathom now.

Who invented those girls? Surely,
not their parents, or a climate
complete with June snow and January fog.

Did you go home
and peer into some old album,
sing in your sleep
a snatch of a song from a hot night in Jamaica?

Me, I had a wild cavorting dream
that started on a train on top of a mountain
and ended in a town in northern Italy.
I woke imagining
taffeta somewhere
rustling under the moon
in the Robin Hood Bay dump,
festal in a merry company of rats,
crackling perhaps with a song once danced to,
empty of a wearer.

Sextet

Dance for Strangers

he was by the far wall   across
the intervening distance (watched by nuns)
I saw him   he was wearing a brown n gold shirt—
resplendent 1972 stripes! when the music hit us
at the same time   percussion beat its way

up through the floor
through our feet
our weak knees, stopping
somewhere just below our wide, vinyl belts,
and well below
our brains where blood
buzzed and danced

it was only a matter of catching his eye

on the floor, bodies bumping us,
I tell myself
don't   look at his hips
        look behind his head   look cool
don't   look
at that zipper winking under a flashing light, pulling
the sightline
toward trouble

we took advantage of nothing more than that
but something got moving: it still
pulses

every time it senses
certain drumbeats—

twenty-two years later, on a Friday night
play me something old and wild and fast
and walk across
that dance-hall-living-room-school-gym floor

and I'll let my eyes go anywhere
anything moving leads me.

The Fashion News

Cover that breast, it offends my eye.
                                        — Molière

See, make a flip-book
of this magazine here
(too flip for words)
take a look:
famines race by;

a Saturday night ritual: the fashion magazine,
a movie you wouldn't like (some slight sex-*tête*)
wine for one:

dots are in
stripes V to navels sucked tight to spines
someone's revived Adidas jogging suits as dresses—
breasts are in
are up
cantilevered, engineered and hammocked—
the better to see the fleshless ribs, my dear,
breasts are up, are out,

are in

i'm in
the steam,
going pink in the heat;
four candles dance light across my breasts
and the water is silky with magnolia

this is the solitary joy of flesh, the secret pleasure
of displacing water, making it rise higher;
all this space I take
is assurance against hunger.

the rest is irrelevant:

what's in   what's out   what's up

Summer Night Heat

too bad you're not here.

Out in the garden, night-scented stock
breathes next to the deck
and the moon
is a suggestion three-quarters full
like me; the night is redolent
with scent... ideas... provocations:
too bad you're not here.

The air flexes masseur's fingers,
awakens tired skin; slit hem
of a sundress funnels the breeze
under;
I read poems with the tips of my fingers,
would massage you with their words,
make you feel their rhythms along your spine:

too bad you're out of town.

Here, for you, is a letter about the night,
composed on air and unsent:
The moon is three-quarters full,
and breezes run. I have Chardonnay and your absence
and other women's words
in the book you gave me.

too bad you're out of town

but no night's a waste;
I will write you the night, save it
for winter, the heat
of one
of our arguments.

I'm Having this Dream on a Train

The drive's the thing, the car
a faster car than any I've owned. Red,
of course. Up winding roads
at the speed of dappled light; all morning
the road is an upward pull to a place
spiced with giant evergreens. Crashing
piano on the stereo, a tumbling eagerness
out the window. Open, of course.
Placid blue sky: peripheral vision sees
white fingers on piano keys, your fingers
across my skin, the red of the car
like some enclosing heat. The cabin appears
deserted: no smoke, no vehicle—are you here?
Yet when I reach the door, it is already opening
outward, and I cannot so much see you

in the sudden
cabin-dark

as sense you:

Pull me inside quickly, just
let me drop this picnic basket;
whatever you are wearing I feel,
soft but unseen;
nothing really between us
but fabric thin as cirrus
and the worn skins
of months of separation.

Notes on the Sexual Division of Labour

So you were there
when the body played out
its eventual nature
its drive

on a long table: my legs were frozen

you were not there—not really:
how could you be?
you saw them cut through me,
so how could you be there; people who witness
such things must be somehow absent.

I had already become a concentration of breath and waiting arms:

had lost two-thirds of my body
to the absence of sensation.
*I might as well be a caryatid
holding this crazy scene up,*
I said to the anaesthetist, but
he was already laughing
at my outrageous reaction
to something as normal as birth:

those legs are marble: they are not mine.

Then out of the dead marble, they lifted
our daughter. She pissed on the doctor
and closed her eyes against
the thousand blazing suns around her.
And two hours later,
her long eyes roving under the shield of a blanket,
I felt the sensation: marble made flesh.

Nights later, you lay next to me, but keeping your distance.

I touched my legs, once marble, felt
the abdominal flesh where nerves were cut
through. It was a long time
before this body wanted anything: night after night

it expressed only a craving for itself.

Dance

I'll be thirty-five this year,
is the kind of thing I say
after new year's, tally:

aching back
thoughts unstrung
too many deadlines
hard week all round, but

it's Friday night and the child
is asleep
following an elaborate ceremony with ritual objects:
cookies, a whirlpool bath and three books,

and the wine tonight is red silk
and the moon through the back window
is a coin I've spent again and again,
and will spend until

there are no moons or windows. Your arm
curving along the sofa is white, smooth,
ageless. And your voice is a kind of hush
with the Atlantic in it; salt and wind
soothing
invigorating
at the same time

and nothing we say much matters,

is merely a bridge across
a river that changes every season, is
a dance floor full of distances and other dancers
crossed again and again, so play

some old music
from the years we danced away from childhood

see what happens.

Love and the Swan

Is it possible to write about love and swans and not be overpowered by Yeats?
—Kenneth Sherman in *Books in Canada*, February 1996.

It was a year when possibilities
of love were splitting, flying out,
particular, in all directions.

"Do you think it's possible to be in love
with two people at once?" he asked.
"This is not love," I said, sure
under the black June sky, not
a star in sight, the rain's
first whispering pish on the ivy leaves
as if a ghost were brushing against the wall
to eavesdrop on some earthly foolishness.

"And that's not love either," I said, speaking
of the other one, the one of two,
his letter folded like origami in my pocket.
"You. Him. You only want to know
where I am all the time."

Romance had worn off me
or been absorbed like old makeup
that day in Stratford-upon-Avon
when I bent to photograph
the question-mark neck, wings like Gabriel's:
my back was stiff from listening half the night.

When the swan attacked, I smelled
bracken in its feet, old weather and decay
in the pockets of its wings
that beat my head;

the photograph is a blur:
a ripple in a pond,
an echo in it of the harsh voice of the swan
dropping a warning in my ear.
Christ, it was a hard year.

Thinking about Washboards

I am thinking about washboards.

Light through the window strikes bottlegreen suncatcher:
how I admired the glint of sun on ridged green glass,
how I would think—*glacier*.

Time in a second can throw me back—
I am leaning over the wooden washtub steaming
chlorine bleach inhalant—
    my sister's diapers
    these Saturday night dance shirts
    socks worn to cross berry bogs
must all come clean:

six-year-old seeks heaven helping mommy

and I learned to love to be victorious, defeat dirt—
my father's shirt collars were wrung
(instead of his neck at times)
into purity. Scrub like a saint.

And nothing changed except the years,
how easily I could reach the new sink. In 1972
I grow spots, plot a fitting end for them,
while I pull the new jeans up and down
those washboard ridges—fade them, age them
before the weekend; dark dyes
won't do for dances with older guys.

Why am I thinking about washboards?

Maybe this high blue March Monday
is the eternal washday
and I saw a woman sucking in her gut on Water Street,
and thought—

—of a high Monday morning
and a once-treasured man saying
    that with a few gut crunches
    say one hundred sit-ups a day
    and some moves derived from fencing
I could have
    a washboard stomach—

I touched my flesh between t-shirt and jeans,
liking its nomad pliability,
looked at our mingled laundry
tussling on the floor
while hot bleach rose and stung my eyes

saw us
far too entangled

on the floor the laundry piled higher and higher,
year upon year, needing to be done,
and I said, "I think you'd better go now."

Better than wringing the necks of his shirts.

This morning, grit lies heavy on the world,
needs a washboard,
a girl's strong hands.

Awake these Nights Dreaming in Colour

not only dreaming in colour
but awake I see you in blue, green
you in a forest somewhere; I am
walking to you from the river
char coal and silver,
and beyond dreaming in colour
I place your skin against grass,
birch bark, moss, comparative
textures:

you are gone:
as surely as out of a dream, strolling
away in black and white, but I'm here, placing you
on a red deck chair on a white beach
light spills the sun, gold into your hair,
the glass in your hands, the sand

then I visit you
in imagined coral rooms, lie
damp against you on claret carpets
and hold your face gone translucently white
under a blue moon and, still unsatisfied,
populate invented rooms
with watchers in velvet hats
and ghostly passersby in shrouds woven of shadows

a penny for your dreams, oblivious you.

I spin out textures, careful in the warp, the weft,
the distinctions between shades of cobalt
(and how they oppose tangerine)
while in the black-and-white night
your fingers twitch, catching nothing
at the ends of your arms, except
a swollen island of pillow and a fold of red quilt
in the shape of a scarab.

Adam and Eve on a Winter Afternoon

Adam comes in from sawing wood
with a chip on his shoulder.
And grunts. And heaves the wood down,
a heavy drop filled with creeping, unsaid things,
to the woodbox.

And Eve is trying to imagine it not there,
that slow and trembling thing within his breath
that lives between inhale and exhale. This
must be just exertion, and yet it feels
like a weapon, not quite secret but concealed.

She has words for such days—*wood hyacinth,
aurora borealis, Harley-Davidson*—either
ethereal beauty or a fast-flying escape.
But the kitchen is a trap baited with supper cooking
and the imminent arrival of children.

And Adam says, "Whas for supper?"
And Eve says, "Soup."
And he says, "Any meat in it?
I hope you're not off meat again. Growing
children need their protein. And this
is no climate to be eating like rabbits."

And then the old clock rescued from a house
where pouncing bargain hunters drove deals at a death sale
hammers four o'clock home.

And Eve thinks that four o'clocks are old-fashioned flowers,
and she stirs the soup and plunks down
in her bentwood rocker with her seed catalogues,
thinks *crocosmia*
thinks *branching tulip*
thinks *Apricot Beauty*
thinks *hemerocallis*

And the ragged thing between breath and breath
is there again, just for a second, a thing of air
with claws and teeth.

And Adam goes out for another load
before the early dark sinks in on him,
and while his saw buzzes
the language of massacre on wood
thinks *tomorrow's Friday*
thinks *pint of Guinness*
thinks *at least she dyed her hair*
thinks *I can hear the children*

Their footsteps saw over frozen grass, their voices
high, inadvertently calling everything back together,
one of them playing a blackbird's call on a recorder.

Aphrodisiacs for a Newfoundland Winter...

If You Enter a Kitchen Smelling of Winter Savoury

Innocent-seeming,
you might find it in the salami,
or steeping deep in the chicken
one winter evening when you enter the kitchen,
innocent-seeming;

if you believe in stories cast by scent
be ready to capitulate,
such is rumoured the power of winter savoury—

and all the ponds are frozen, love
nowhere to find the antidote—
white water lilies, *Nymphaea alba*,
their cool bodies rising from still pools;
all the ponds are frozen, heart of winter—
nothing now to cool the ardour

of kitchens and their smells
and what might well be spells.

This Happened with Strawberries

Because she dreamed summer came into a dark room,
charged the wind with assault and battery,
charged the rain with break and entry,
and made them leave her alone,

Because summer entered her in a dream,
made the seasons spin
madly out of order
and placed in her mouth a ruby sweetness;

Because he became for her summer
that moment he entered the room,
carrying a basket of strawberries,
and everything she hated vanished in him.

This happened with strawberries
because of a dream, a cold day
and something he saw in a store window
that reminded him of late summer hay
and the scent of her hair on a pillow.

Eschewing Oysters, He Brought Her a Fish

When he knocked on the door, and she answered, light spilled out and he felt, suddenly, exposed. He tried to say something about how hard it was to get anything fresh in the depths of winter, but ended by telling her a long rambling story of a day by a hole in the ice, waiting, waiting for a fish to fly up, and give him an excuse to visit her.

He had wrapped the char in paper, and he pulled it back, just a little, to show her he had a valid excuse, and she said, "I have a lemon for it. Thanks. Come on in out of the cold." But he was unnerved by the light that spilled from the house, and all it spoke to him of private spaces.

Later, as she peeled back the silvered skin, savoured every morsel on her tongue, she tasted his day, felt the dry wind on his cheeks, the stiffness of his hands, felt the waiting, as if he had filled the fish with his longing and fed it to her. She sat in her dark front room, looked out to where the moon silvered the frozen lake, could think of nothing but bringing him in, out of the dark, the cold, and to her.

Sweet Anise

Not exactly something
you'd find sprouting
from a hoary bog,
licorice-scented,
carrying breaths of winds
from places that know no winter.

It spread a rumour
in Greece, Rome and Asia Minor
of strengthening powers,
nights that stretched, sweet successes.

It was known also
to sweeten the breath,
cure flatulence,
fight giddiness and nausea and shooting pains,
and do so many things
that surely made the course of love run smoother.

What lesson there? Perhaps only a suggestion
to ask one's love,
"What ails you? How can I make it better?"

Oh, to be such a cure, so varied and healing,
humble and versatile as a herb
with a reputation for pleasing!

Baked in Chocolate

Knowing that the ground horns of dead things
and nettles gathered in wildernesses had no power,
she took the moon instead and baked it in chocolate.

Knowing that three ancient words chanted
while a herb lay tied in ribbon under a pillow
had no power, she took a saxophone solo,
baked it in chocolate.

Knowing that after Christmas, there is only winter
for too long without relief or light, she took a June night,
baked it in chocolate.

Her lover praised the cake, dreamt off after supper
to walk under a moon on a night too strangely warm
for a jacket, only thought of returning home
when the saddest notes broke out of a third-floor window.

Sprouting House

Seedlings long for the sun's fire.
Peat pots feel the deep weight
oppressing them; barometer falling, falling:
wet-northeast-Atlantic- April.

This house is so wet
its very foundations are greening; moss
overtakes emerging grass
in verdant sidewalk cracks: imagine
if you were small enough, antlike,
the landscape within them.

This morning when the rain
came down again, tapping
the roof, stroking the eaves,
I felt the house sink, and then,
a rising sensation of maybe germination.

Could this house be sprouting?
I imagine it developing leaves, tendrils
curling, slapping at windows during endless winds,
eventually breaking them, invading rooms,
the carpets greening, our footsteps
and our loud unnerved voices
becoming soft and never echoing.

By summer, the neighbours have stopped
talking; everything in this world
is but a seven days' wonder, and nothing
under the sun or rain is new.

We sleep now, most of the time, our limbs
earthy, our hair fronds.
Friends wonder whether this house
has become our grave, or whether
we had always been merely seeds, waiting
to sprout lives, voices.

Floating

1.

In our neighbour's house
the atmosphere surely must have been water,
for I kept floating out of my chair
up,
up, up
toward the ceiling, the beam
approaching quickly; I bumped it and felt nothing.

Regina said the rosary. Her daughter, Selina
of the lilting undeveloped voice,
sang the Sorrowful Mysteries
as if they were country tunes,
and the Joyful Mysteries like ribald shanties
from last night at the Patrick's Day concert.

Up now as far as I could go, I used to think
the moon was pulling me up to meet it.

When I was young, they gave me
bread and jam to keep me quiet.
When I got older, they gave me
silence: same effect.

But all those evenings they made
the Glory Be To The Father sing
as if it were made to dance to.

2.

I lost the gift.
The body got heavier and could not do the trick,
although I tried to rise on a cushion of narcotic, to float
myself to the high beams
while the moon rose through the window.

I thought of them there where the river sang
through the long, green evenings
through all the hushes between the words

where Regina and Selina died each night, convinced
of the imminent end of things,
and rose each morning grateful for survival.

3.

Insomnia is a gift now.
The baby inside me floats up at night
from body to consciousness;
no longer a fishy amorphous thing,
she has whispered to me her gender.

Somebody with eyes, hands, impulses,
messages pumping through the blood.
To make her settle, I touch the spot where now she stirs,
but she is up.

With the inward eye, I see her hair
wet and shining like precious metal,
and eyes of agate, jade or tourmaline,
carnelian or sardonyx, flashing
and changing like river stones,
their brightnesses ascending.

Guardian

First there were saints;
first, angels.

Michael pressed himself against the bedroom door,
held it tight against Lucifer,
and asked nothing more.

Gabriel brought the mail.

Francis fed birds in the garden;

Stephen died for me.

Christopher carried me
over Barasway bridge,
safely
through the lightning
in a car so old only a saint would trust it.

Jude pitied me.

The word was made flesh. Saints
become men in a girl's religion.

The young mechanic
apologizing for his nails,
saying love you, love you...
offering a charm bracelet.

The leaping acrobat.

The man who crossed an ocean
to confess in a bar.

The poet styled after an early martyr,
nearly causing a saint-swoon in me.

And each brought that word, as if he alone
had battled demons for it—
love.
I love
your hair. I love
the smell of trees
after rain, the bark is your body.
I love
thick and thin and red and green
and, of course, you.

As surely as angels fall,
everything turns to its obverse.
The dropping off
of care, the coming of cold; we give
into each other's demands
like mutual hostages
to be trapped
together in this room
where, curiously, I find myself alone.

And, arriving here, I'm amazed I've come so far
to the flesh-destiny of new creation,
to a small, sleeping life
which I must serve
as saint of multiple purposes,
while, outside, voices
unidentified, as if
of a new world barely born
whisper in the thin rain of September.

The Way You Walk into the Water

as if a warmth like sudden
waves of heat awaking buds
had suddenly found you

and said, "Bloom!"
you walk into the water
and your ankles blossom purple

as if turquoise wavelets lapped
your feet, and this was Santorini

as if this cold is all the oceans you will know
(and what else is innocence?)
your body draws itself together;
fists clench and you dance
a shiver-dance and call

"Come in," you say, "it's beautiful, brrr,"
in the shrill voice of a shorebird,
blooming there, strange marine iris,
my anemone, my urchin.

three   balloons   on   a   wall

three balloons on   your bedroom wall   horizontal traffic lights:

not

    yellow-red-green

but

    yellow-green-blue

not

    caution-stop-go

but

    what?

this sky balloon compelling you

beyond caution   beyond go,

to?

later in real traffic you say

yellow means be careful   green means go   blue means fly

Among the Shadows of Everything

Saturday, so we go to the park for something to do.
A hill to slide on, an icy pond of dripline freeze
for a quick skate on winter boots

under the afterimages of leaves
that hang, ghostlike, from the trees.

A day such as this,
frozen   still
hangs,
connective tissue between
past
        and future,

                a time
to look for the warm heart
of winter, the hot, parched
core of rain, the stillness within
the flapping V of migrating birds,
and the sound
of winter
   melting,
   water
   falling;
even as freeze sets in, it is breaking.

Love, we have learned, spreads itself
in malls, garages and cathedrals
when people enter them; whenever
my daughter and I go looking,
looking
to pass the time away,
we feel the same
pulse,
see the same
lines and curves and arcs
repeated, not to infinity,
but as far as we can see
                ahead.

See the end already there
in the beginning,
   the beginning   with its hope
—vivid and illimitable—
resting in a foregone conclusion;

such sights are the wellsprings
of sorrow and of dreams:

this juncture

between the quick collecting of cells
and their dispersal, like seeds
in their own sweet time,
one moment
when messages are encoded
to balance

and life lies still,
swung
    in a hammock,
      doing nothing
to begin or end itself, observing
the play of light on a screen
suspended
     in the air—what's there besides that great grey sky?

Whatever this stillness is, she feels it too.

Her small boots stick
in their footsteps, and she says, "Grrr.
A great big bear is coming
to knock down all the trees.   Grrr."
Mittened hands raised, she threatens a leaning pine

and sees the bear coming again and again
among the shadows of everything

past summers with their lucid rain,
winters in a maddening cycle,   whistling winds

she stops sometimes, looks at the sky,
and sighs;
          and if it is possible to perceive
the shifts of last year's light in afterimage,
is it not also possible to see foreshadows?

and the burden of her first knowledge of death
in this, her fifth year, swells like a damp seed inside her.

"C'mon," I say, "It's cold."
I conjure hot chocolate, a framed view
of juncos at the feeder, a favourite film
that will play again and again, often
as we want it to.   I stamp my feet,
she stamps her feet: we pound the rigid earth.
We do not look   into the hugeness of the sky.

Early Acquaintance

In a dreaming world, you were
a floating eye

an egg you say now

I saw you as eye, turning to observe
its own fast collecting of cells

into a body

yourself you say now

but then it was only the first
ripe day of our acquaintance;
the sun, when I left the clinic,
was wheeling like a yellow gull
over the harbour, my head was full
of the sounds of the day, the traffic
of the city drove completely through me,
and every smell is yet engraved on my memory

so this is how we got to know one another:
I phoned everyone, almost wrecked the car,
bought vitamins, threw my cigarettes
on the floor and stomped on them, saw in my mind
a long chain of life stretching
endlessly back and ahead

when I was just a little egg,
you said the other day
I was just a little egg.

but in me you were already someone
who, inhabiting me, was making me a world
complete with seas and soft valleys and mountains
pushing to the surface, the splitting
of cells creating continents

in the beginning of time, you were
the unspecialized mass, but coded for everything:

someone has told you you were a seed:
what does this make you see—

I the green land, medium for growing
turf on the edge of a cliff
at the edge of the sea, eyes to the horizon

watching a wrinkle on the ocean from where the past had come,
tossed up like flotsam.

We were none of those things that day
and I knew it,
went home and lay down, too wild to go anywhere,
too dangerous for words.

Anthemic

Our best and brightest are leaving in droves

is what they've been saying all summer—
rough choruses
of pundits and doomsday prophets

dying for the millennium

the same refrain like a shanty
sung in a bar at closing time

sound over meaning.

And yet
my child's caramel hair
is spun gold by the evening sun,
old alchemy from a tale of princesses and deadlines.

She traverses a crackling path of Wedgwood mussel shells
to a hiding place of secreted treasures tossed up by the pirate currents:

all day she's been singing "that beautiful song"
carried on the wind from a pageant: now, a wisp
of voice curls back at me, "God guard thee, Newfoundland."

The sky opens, pulled apart by light, casting over dark hills
shades of coral, mauve, citrine and then

a blue as still as a final decision.

Across Trinity harbour, lights twinkle on
and first stars signal back; on the sea side
the moon is up:

leviathan backs rise from an evening fog—the whales
are singing, continuing through the night

a kind of anthem.

de Chirico's girl doesn't sleep all night

all the real I can summon tonight,
the howling, wet February wind
the quiet lapping of a child's sleep
on the throbbing remains of a headache:
nothing can relieve the sense of a precipice
from which I will certainly fall
if I sleep.

in the book I'm flipping through
in the nowhere middle of the night,
as if night had a middle,
there's "Melancholy and Mystery of a Street";
de Chirico's girl with flying hair
rolls her hoop
down a narrow yellow track between
arcaded buildings, down
the tilt-a-whirl piazza
where the shadowed figure, shadowed spike
waits.

the hoop through the headache clangs
loud as the hoops I rolled
down the dusty track to Branch gut;
and, having rolled hoops,
I want to stop her, tell her
that even if she passes the shadow,
beyond the street lies waiting the long cliff-fall,
the precipice at the end of all sleep.

outside the dangerous kitchen window
which tries to present itself as a black wall
lie the barely discerned fingers
of rocking, moaning trees, and the wet wind
pulling at a single star, and beyond the shed,
there is only the ear-recognition
of a dog's bark, nothing to be seen.

the window glass shakes and bends;
for a second I see
myself, the book, the lamp, the girl
all flung outside. Then, like a bird settling
in the still, interior branches of a tree,
a silence comes
beyond reckless flight or fear or vertigo.

How She Had Her Nervous Breakdown

She was standing by the dryer when the end-of-cycle timer went off. Rising, ears offended, she heard the call of church bells in the other ear or air, and a siren far away, faint as a kettle's first whistle, but heavy as damage, then all sounds blending into an alarm, a call. That

afternoon, walking in a mall in search of the world's warmest sweater and three pairs of children's sneakers, she dreamed of alone by a coddled fire, though her house had no fireplace, and she smoked a cigarette with such intensity, a man looking for a light had to say "excuse me" three times before she pulled her eyes away from the merging greenness the leaves on the potted trees had become, and saw his features
swing
into place,
like puzzle pieces shuffled.

Later, waiting in the yard in front of the elementary school, fleeting things moved at the outer edges of her vision, and she tried to place them, name them, but a buzzer rang, and children, including two of her own, swarmed toward her. In the car, the boy waved his small fingers in front of her face, "Hullo, anybody home?" After

a weekend when sauces stuck to pots and silences grew monstrous, she sat in the doctor's office and said, "I can't remember driving anywhere."

Left with a prescription for dreamless sleep, a scrunched booklet, and another, slightly embarrassing appointment, then stood and looked at the park,
the harbour,
the small shops,
saw how everything was made of waves that might at any moment shift,
ripple
like stage curtains in a magic show,
and re-form
into a scene entirely unknowable and unfamiliar.

For the First Time in Months, She Feels Her Feet

He was always going to look after them
until he went out one day
too far for his boat and the weather,
making all questions rhetorical,
whether he would change,
would go to the store for diapers
or cook meals, would keep loving
his wife's sister. Full fathom five
and it's all over, but wind whipping
on this icy slope; he tried to do too much,
then his boots got full and pulled him under.

She strokes her boy's hair;
absent fingers pull out strands
without even knowing, and the boy
must be grateful for the pain taking him out
of the trance state where his eyes stare
so hard that the hill divides
into pinpoints of light and colour
hard to put back together,
even that rose of blood on the snow
where the nail dug into his finger.

Later, she realizes that she can feel
the squish of water that tells her
her boots have soaked, and she feels
her feet for the first time in months,
and worries suddenly
that the boy will catch cold,
she pulls their eyes away from the hill,
their feet, towards town.
On the way down, she remembers the first time he hit her.

The Cat Is Dead; Long Live the Cat

She came and sat on the bed in the half light of morning.
She was the same but winged—strange
diaphanous accessories; delicate for a cat,
but perfect for a cat so vain.

Her shadow, now, passes me
once or twice a day on the stairs; I call her
the furtive upstairs maid, always
brushing quietly in a corner.

Kidney disease: after twelve years
of traipsing laps, belle
of dinner parties, feline
reincarnation of a flapper,
it came down to:

could she and I take another day of her life, or
could I hold her while a needle stopped her heart?

She'd lived long enough for vets to stop running tabs;
please pay with your Visa or MasterCard; six weeks later
the bill comes: *You're still with us*, I call
to her ghost upstairs, *The cat is dead; long live the cat*!
No reply but a faint rubbing at a spot on the carpet.

Then it was a very quiet fall,
an autumn of silences and felt ghosts, until
a November night in the car, my stoic child spills
like the broken sky. *I want her back. There's no god,
is there? If there was, he'd know how I feel and send her back—*

In the glove compartment, a brochure
Saying Goodbye to Your Animal Companion—

I've buried four grandparents, and am always
finding death for the first time,
a cat in my arms above a steel table,
a car at a red light, a child
pitching forward through life
to a hole she sees yawning at the end of it.

Winter has a way of freezing sorrow,
stilling it like water iced; some nights
there's a scratching at the window, the sudden fear
I've locked someone out
on such a cold night.

If I Could Give You Now

What I remember of you
is the very smallness of your wrists,
how the slightness of your body
made it dance like a stalk of grass in each small wind

and, oh, how we danced when the wind was wild and high,
blowing our traded secrets out over the bay!

You still believed
that a fat and magic man with twinkling eyes
and scads of gifts existed, loved you,
although there were compartments of your innocence
that had been invaded, then closed for(almost)ever.

And I never knew then I would break your heart,
telling you that Santa Claus was not what you thought
was a mother—not
a father, surely. For fathers
were the lords-a-leaping, drunk
for most of the twelve days of Christmas.

In return, you told me how women and men had sex,
making a circle and a kind of poker with your thin fingers:
"Nah, it'd crack off," I said,
and tried to draw it with a compass and protractor,
but none of the angles were persuasive. And how
did you know
such impossible things were possible?

Because someone had already tried
to show you how it worked
and wanted you to work it.

Age nine:

it seems so far away now; I never knew then
that when I said,
"Santa Claus is your mother,"
I broke into the final place in your heart
that held out hope for magic
and belief
in a being
who, unlike Jesus and his vaporous angels,
knew how to make a kindly presence felt.

If I could give you now
what was taken away then,
I would—

would fill the meadows with angels bearing gifts
and populate the stars
with strange bright beings,
your name and love burning on their lips.

Let Us Go and Find a Place of Worship

At a quarter to eleven
on an ordinary Wednesday
the church bells have been ringing
clear in the clarion-carrying air
for five full minutes—
what is this,
another death or what is going on?

Above the houses across the street
fawn-coloured branches scratch
stiffly, arthritically
at pigeon-coloured clouds,
try to scrape them
off the blue beyond, the hidden
sky over sky.

Keep the taps running, you said:
this recent rain has merely driven
the frost deeper underground;
two hundred households have awakened
to empty pipes singing the absence of water.

Veering toward St. Patrick's Church,
two ancient women are walking uphill,
their backs bent to hold the grade inside themselves
as balance. Thick, I wonder how
they can walk on legs as slim as twigs
and still hold that hill
so placidly inside their hips.

I hear your breath
between the peals of bells—
almost in hibernation, your sleeping voice
occupies the space between weekday pilgrims' steps.
You say you have no need for these sharp mornings,
for revelations to rouse you.

But let us go and find
a place of worship; something is stirring,
perhaps the ground-breaking of the spring
echoing through basements, or the tremor
that shakes the dormancy of seeds, wakes
them from a dream of their own brief flowering.

I wish you could hear yourself.
In the room where you wait
this frozen season out,
your every breath is a longing for summer.

Breaking Ice

A man is breaking ice outside his front door which faces east and somewhat north. That front door faces only the promise of the sun; the sun itself gone by morning half-time so that the ice builds and builds, pushing toward April.

She says, "You need a pick to do that," but he only has a shovel, and so he pounds its blunt tip into the ice. Brilliant three-dimensional sparks fly out. She thinks mortar and pestle; thinks sorrow is what makes us work.

He pounds his sadness to dust, grinds her silence to powder, grinds woody ice-locked stems to *fines herbes* while the day fades to black.

They have talked already of when to tell the children.

But today they work like all work is waiting, and waiting is all work. Mortar and pestle. He grinds ice to shimmering dust, dreams of the grapefruit league and sees a white ball sailing through Florida's azure heaven. And she...

And she pries ice from thyme in the back garden. The sun warms her back and gives her hair red highlights that she can see when she bends over. Somewhere a ball slices the air, dividing the season into the dead winter / the new spring. There is less ice here out back. The garden faces southwest.

Dappled

This morning, all
is a play of light and shadow,
dark and light dancing
in the same flower,
its green, its pink
both light and dark;

our eyes shift or the light
itself does, a white butterfly
going suddenly grey or cream
in the dappled inner spaces
of *dicentra's* hanging hearts:

here, we have no straight answers
no sure, true arrows of certainty
to pin this garden
where and how it is, and this
is how we come to know
the little we do about the world.

The phone will ring, three sharp alarms
and I will not touch it; someone will require
a straight answer
to a simple question. What could I send
through the quivering, expectant silence?
Not this shifting play,
this dappled truth.